by Ros Asquith.

PANDORA

LONDON SYDNEY WELLINGTON

First published by Pandora Press, an imprint of the Trade Division of Unwin Hyman Limited, in 1989.

© Ros Asquith, 1989

Pandora Press
Unwin Hyman Limited
15-17 Broadwick Street
London W1V 1FP

Unwin Hyman Inc
8 Winchester Place, Winchester, MA 01890, USA

Allen & Unwin Australia Pty Ltd
8 Napier Street, North Sydney, NSW 2060, Australia

Allen & Unwin New Zealand Pty Ltd with the Port Nicholson Press
Compusales Building, 75 Ghuznee Street, Wellington, New Zealand

British Library Cataloguing in Publication Data

Asquith, Ros
    Toddler
    1. English humorous cartoons-collections from individual artists
    1. Title
    741.5'942

ISBN 0-04-440525-1

Typeset in Times by Rowland Phototypesetting (London) Ltd
Printed in Great Britain by Guernsey Press Co, Guernsey, Channel Islands

Contents.......

To Fred, Bill, Jack, Nicola, Cameron, Logan, Jesse, Lily, Alex, Sophie and......

Ros Asquith is a freelance journalist and illustrator living in London. She has been theatre critic for *Time Out* and *The Observer* as well as co-theatre editor of *City Limits* where she still works. She has painted murals in six different countries – and several children's bedrooms. She has a regular weekly cartoon in *The Guardian*. *BABY!* was her first collection of cartoons and *TODDLER!* is the sequel.

By the same author

BABY!

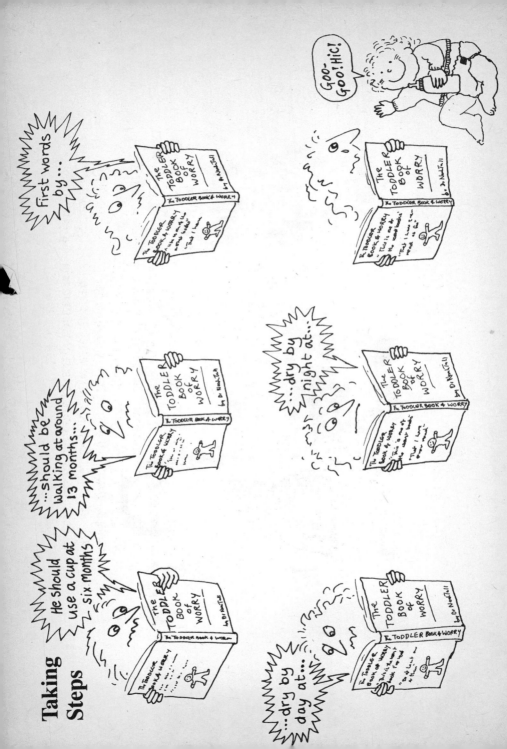

'Bit _old_ for a dummy, isn't he?'

Do not overestimate the abilities of the age group . . . .

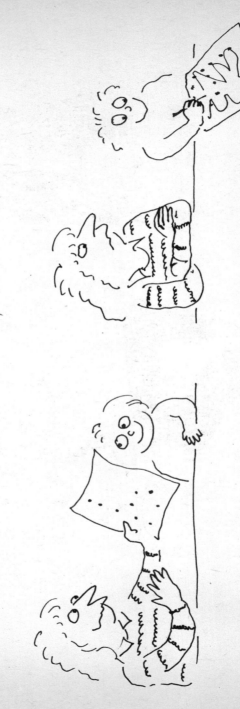

'How about joining up the dots to make a "b"?'

'Let's make a card for grand-pa'

'Or a nice jigsaw?'

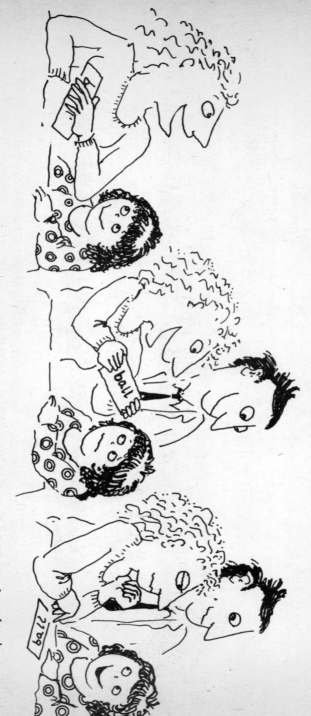

'Darling! Come and see this! She can read'   'Now, what does it say?'   'It sez bog-bog'

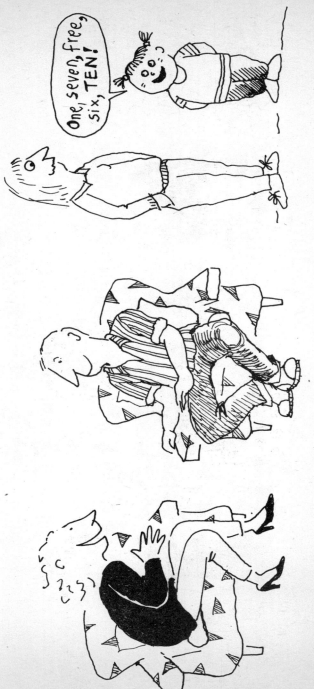

'But of course he's talking! He's got loads of words. "Goonya" means "Ball", "Zob" means "juice", "Mmga" means "Teddy", "Doo-doo" means "Shoe".'

Lies all lies . . .

'Of course, Lucy was walking at 10 months . . .'

'. . . they say that's a sign of high IQ – but I'm sure there's nothing in it'

'Oh, stop worrying so much . . . Ivon never said anything but "no" till he was two and a half and he got a scholarship to Oxford'

'Joshua said "Dada", "Mama" and "ball" at six months . . . of course, it's only because he's <u>unusually bright'</u>

Pictures marked 'a' show the child at home. Pictures marked 'b' show the child during developmental tests at the health clinic.

'Little Oliver not walking yet? I could have sworn he was older than Sophie'

12

'Quick! He's walking!'

'No wonder they cry . . . how would you like to be three foot tall, constantly falling over, flat broke and unable to speak the language.'

To Pee, or not to Pee

'I'm thrilled she's started to use the potty'

Your toddler will play happily for hours . . .

. . . until the phone rings.

'Still in nappies?
But of course boys *are* slower than girls . . . .'

'Er, have you anything *bigger*?'

What's sweet at home may baffle nursery teachers.

A good Scottish phrase, but might it induce a peculiar perception of work?

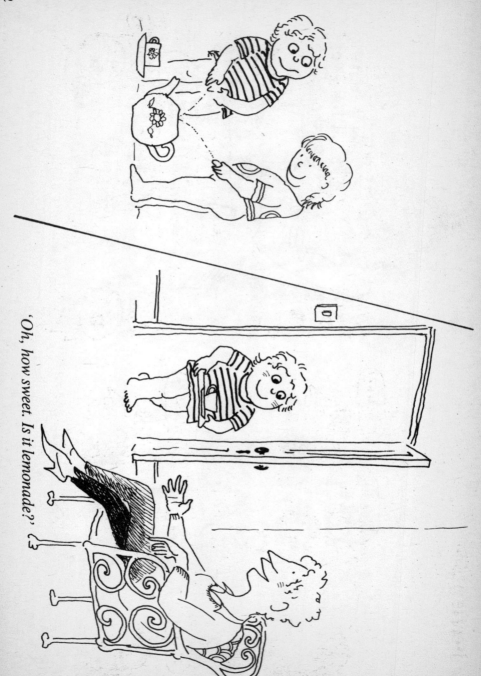

'Oh, how sweet. Is it lemonade?'

Beetle Juice

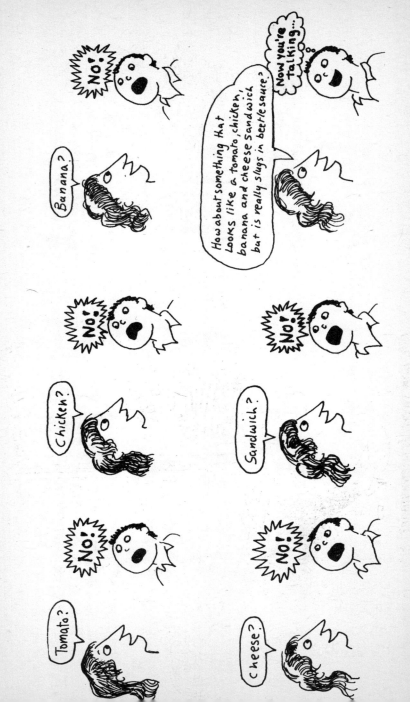

It is ESSENTIAL that your child eats a good mixed diet
The TODDLER BOOK of WORRY by A. Cliché

Well, I suppose a packet of crisps, six chocolate buttons, half a fish finger, a spoonful of peas and a lolly IS mixed...
The TODDLER BOOK of WORRY by A. Cliché

You might try wiles . . .

'You can have another green bean if you've been very very _good_'

'No! No spinach till you've finished all your ice cream!'

'Actually, it's vegetable pie – but I covered it in butter icing'

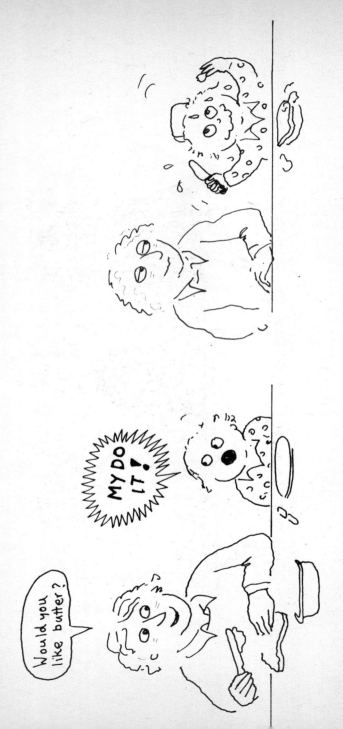

There's a Monster in my Soup

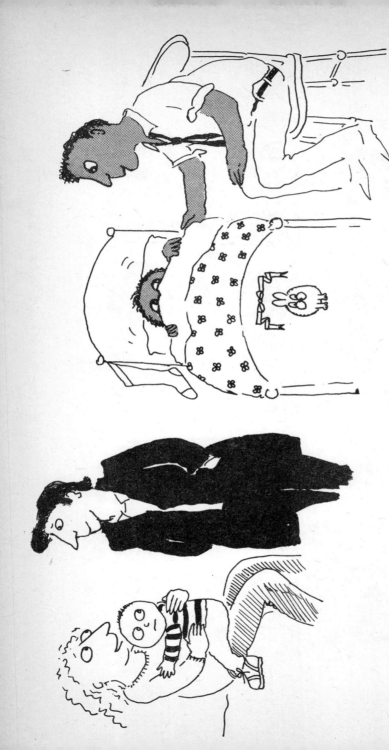

'I know Father Christmas is a big stranger with a beard who comes into your room in the middle of the night. But he's a very kind man . . .'

'I'm not sure he's ready for pantomime – he was scared of Sooty . . .'

'Want to stroke that big pussy-cat'

The same child . . . .

Laugh? I Nearly Died

'Why dat man got no hair?'

'Why dat lady in a BUGGY?'

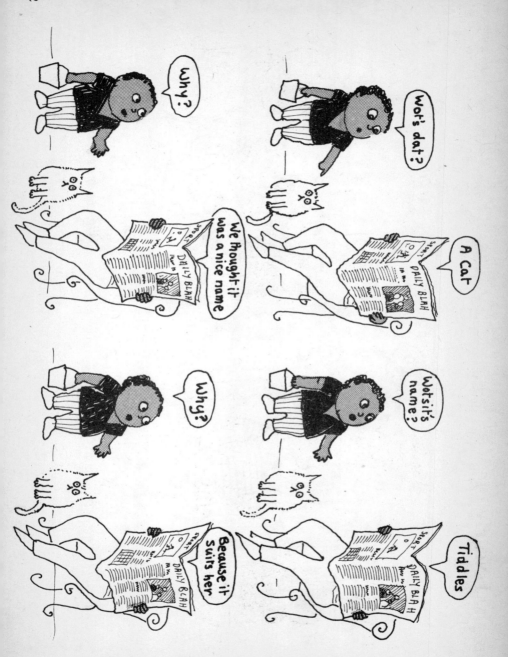

'Dat man VERY FAT. Has he got a baby in his tummy?'

NB *Gordon is one of Thomas the Tank engine's best friends . . . .*

A little knowledge is an awesome thing . . .

'Hello, how do you do?
Pleased to make your
acquaintance.
I'm Amelia Louise Perkins
aged 18 months.
What's your name?'

'S'not electric – it's diesel!'

Where did I come from, Mum?
Well dear, Daddy put a little seed in Mummy and blah blah blah blah blah blah
That's funny. Bill came from Oxford

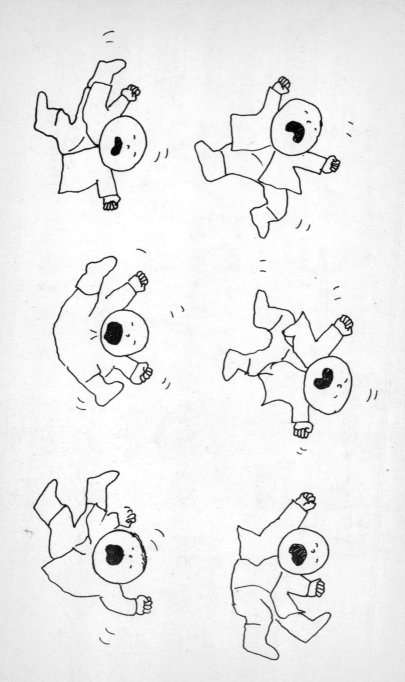

A Whim of Iron

'I only asked him to put on his hat'

Sometimes, you may follow suit . . . .

'Well, WHY isn't there a TANIA the tank engine? Or a HENRIETTA the helicopter? Or an express train called GEORGINA????'

48

49

Avoid asking questions where possible . . .

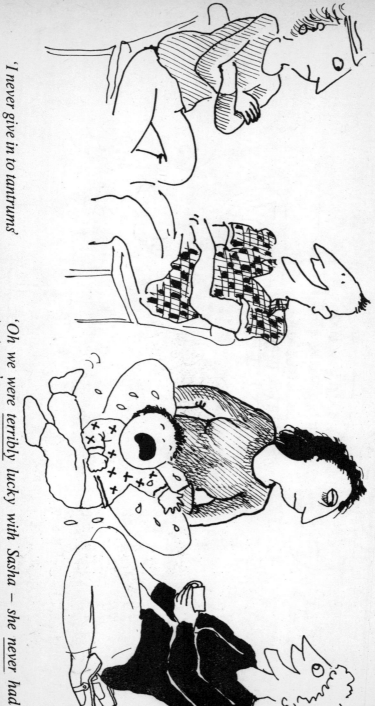

Lies all lies . . . .

'I never give in to tantrums'

'Oh we were terribly lucky with Sasha — she never had tantrums'

Minders

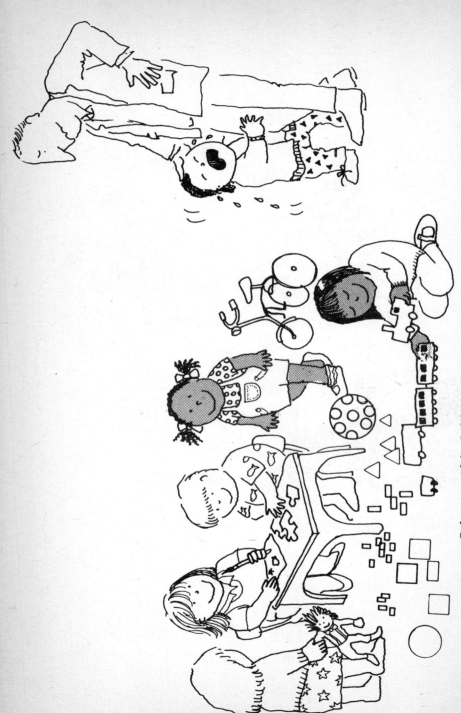

Other people's children settle quickly at playgroup . . . .

'Time for playgroup . . . '

'But I've been. I went _yesterday_!'

Check out your childminders . . .

'Now don't you go walking all over my nice clean floor!'

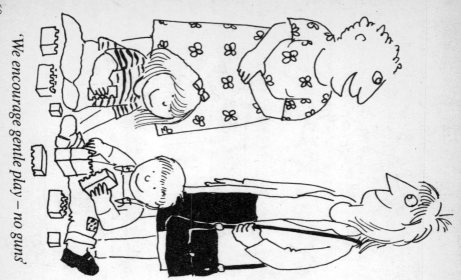

'We encourage gentle play – no guns'

Or you could take out a mortgage . . .

And when you do get a babysitter . . .

Try to leave the kid at home . . .

'Here's a list of things to do if she wakes up'

'And then he peed in my face!'

Dreams and Nightmares

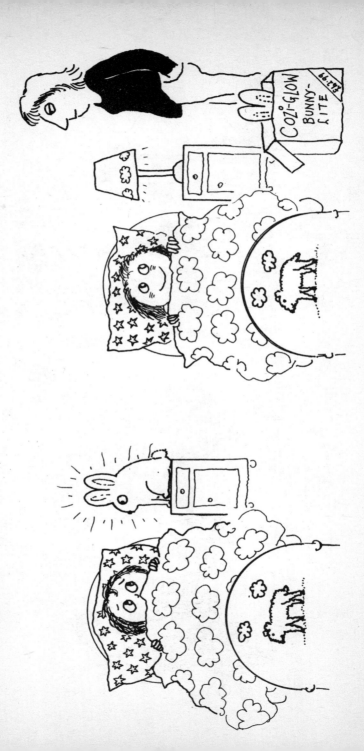

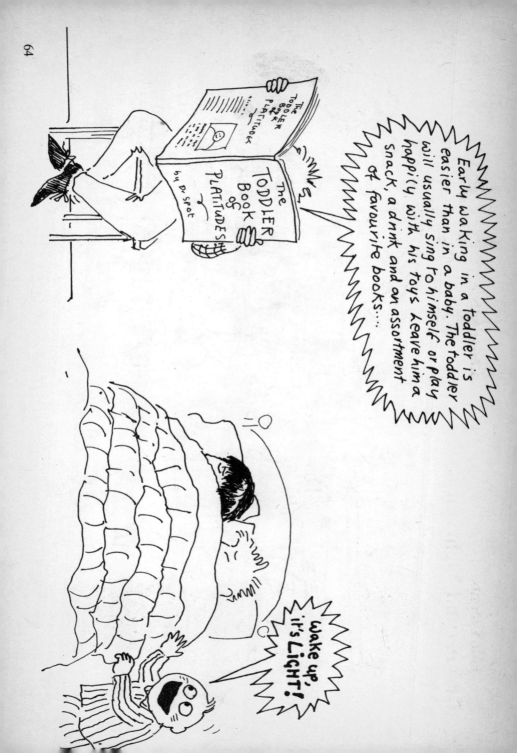

Good nights . . .

Bad nights . . .

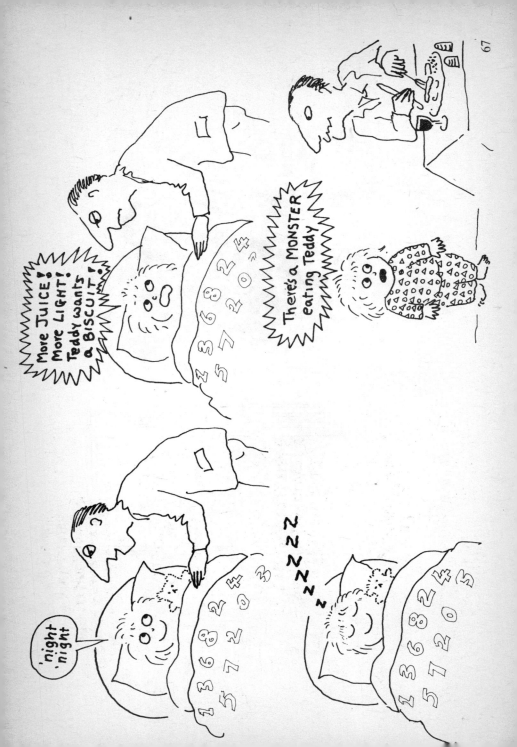

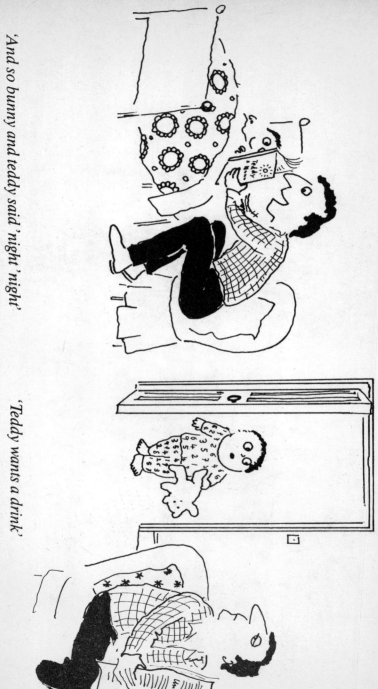

'And so bunny and teddy said 'night 'night'

'Teddy wants a drink'

They will notice if you skip bits . . .

'So the dragon climbed the stairs'

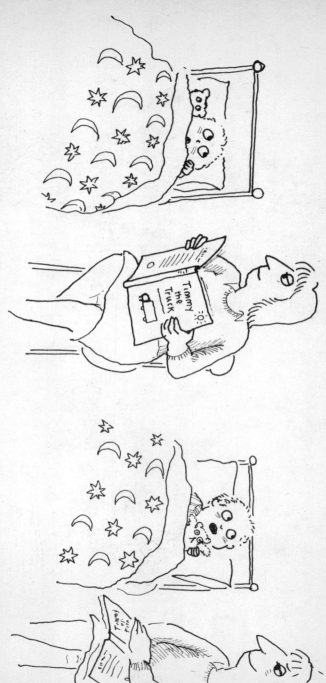

Sibling Ribaldry

'But we don't really <u>need</u> a baby, do we mum? We've got a cat'

'Well then, can I have a bottle? And a dummy? And a nappy?'

'When the baby comes out, I can play with it – and then I can put it back'

71

'But you said she needed a barf!'

'I's jus' bringin' her downstairs'

Try to see things from your toddler's viewpoint . . . .

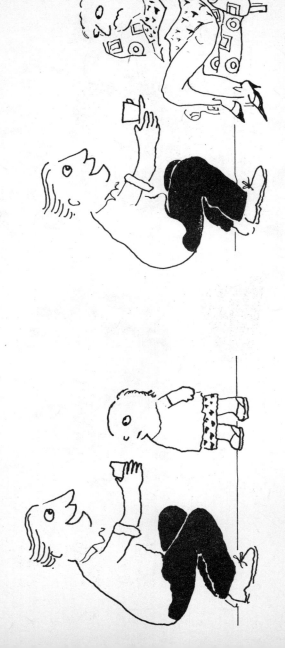

'We love you so much, we're going to have another little baby'

'I love you so much, I'm going to get another younger wife'

74

'I shall really need you, my big boy, to help me look after the new baby'

'I shall really need you, my old husband, to help me look after my young new one'

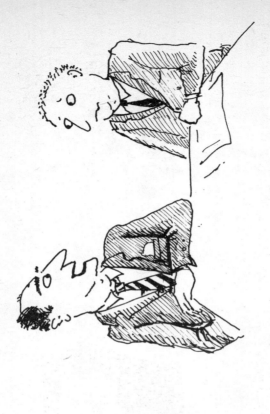

''Fraid we've sold the company to Lord Snooty and his pals, old chap. But I gather they're decent fellows – and I doubt your job will change much'

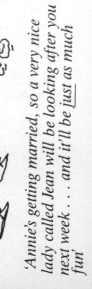

'Annie's getting married, so a very nice lady called Jean will be looking after you next week . . . and it'll be just as much fun'

'Why don't you lend Sam your train?'

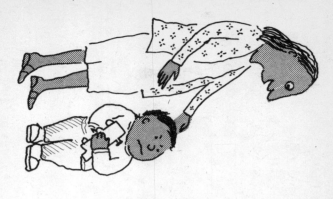

'Why don't you lend Sam's mummy
your compact disc player?'

Partytime

The present . . . .

The arrival . . . .

The games . . .

The departure....

The tea....

The departure....

The tea....

So then he said 'see you soon'
mmmm
I mean what's that supposed to mean? How soon is soon?
Mum?
Should I ring him, do you think?
Um
Mum
Or do you think it's better to play it cool
Um-er
MUM!

You see, I really do rely on your advice
MUM!
I mean I can't bear to think it was just a one-night stand...
Well what would you do? You always seem to know...
He's very DEMANDING for a 3 yr old

It's amazing how many guns can be found around a house . . .

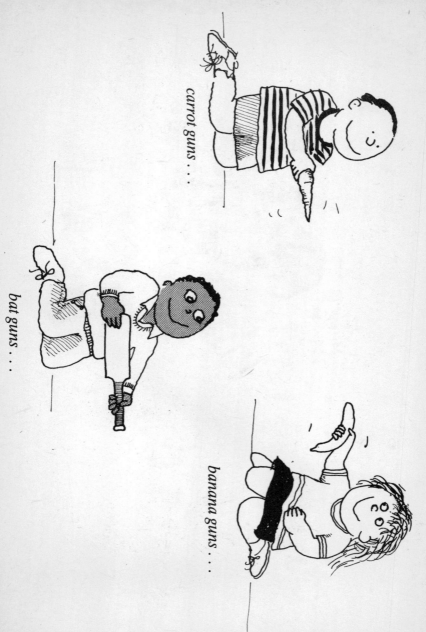

carrot guns . . .

bat guns . . .

banana guns . . .

and, oh no, teddy guns.

pencil guns . . .

Isn't it LOVELY to see boys playing with dolls ...and girls as cowboys

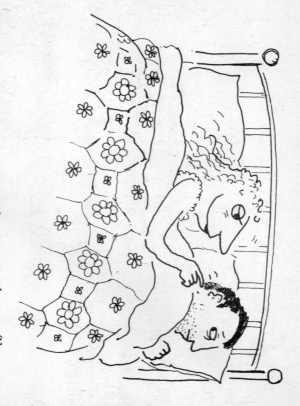

'*Wouldn't it be nice to have a couple more?*'

'We'll have to cancel everyone – it's chicken-pox!'

Coming Soon...Schools...Acne...

Showing Nationwide at a house near you!